101+ Ways to Tell When the Relationship is Over

101+ Ways to Tell When the Relationship is Over

Jeff Hodge

iUniverse, Inc.
New York Lincoln Shanghai

101+ Ways to Tell When the Relationship is Over

iUniverse books may be ordered through booksellers or by contacting:

iUniverse
2021 Pine Lake Road, Suite 100
Lincoln, NE 68512
www.iuniverse.com
1-800-Authors (1-800-288-4677)

First Edition
Text © 2006 by Jeff Hodge
Jokes © Anonymous Authors
Illustrations © Angel D'Amico
Author's photgraph © Val Gelineau

ISBN-13: 978-0-595-42567-9 (pbk)
ISBN-13: 978-0-595-86896-4 (ebk)
ISBN-10: 0-595-42567-4 (pbk)
ISBN-10: 0-595-86896-7 (ebk)

Printed in the United States of America

This book is dedicated to Celia and Jaiden. Love Always.

Contents

Acknowledgments

Thanks:

Jackie Rachal, Beth Ann Meyers, Vanessa Moise, Lauren "Bro. Wack" Gumbs, Romona Carter, Tina Strange, Cedric "Hollywood" Robinson, Mike Jackson, Amanda Cooper, Gabriella Wright, Linnie Wheeles, Alice Fuller, Toni Nettles and Khari Wyatt.

Special Thanks:

To all my ex-girlfriends. Thanks for all the material for this book.

Extra Special Thanks:

To my family for all your love and support throughout the years.

Big Shout-Outs:

To Denver "Spence" Williams, Francis "Big Fran" Acquaye, Kelvin "Wobbly" Hodge, Edgar Hodge and "Jamming" Wayne Williams up in Toronto. Ambassadors of Comedy, thanks for all the jokes. You guys are too funny (www.ambassadorsofcomedy.com).

Introduction

Ok ladies, here is another book for you. Too many times, I meet women who say things like, "How can you tell when a guy doesn't want to be with you anymore?" Instead of having to repeat myself every time I am asked this question, I have decided to write everything down in this book.

Like my previous book, 101+ Ways To Keep A Man, I have decided to keep the mood light by including some of my favorite street jokes I have heard or read over the years. All the jokes are relationship related, so they make the book entertaining as well as informative. On the next page is an example of how men think and stick together.

That's What Friends Are For

Friendship among women:

A woman doesn't come home one night. The next day she tells her husband she slept over at a friend's house. The man calls his wife's ten best friends. None of them know about it.

Friendship among men:

A man doesn't come home one night. The next day he tells his wife he slept over at a friend's house. The woman calls her husband's ten best friends. Eight of them say he did sleep over and two claim he's still there.

1. His penis is raw from having too much sex (and it wasn't with you).

2. He gives you an STD (sexually transmitted disease).

3. There is a used condom in the waste-basket (and it's not yours).

4. There are two empty cocktail glasses in the kitchen sink and one of them has lipstick on it (and the lipstick isn't yours)

Area 51

Late one afternoon, the Air Force folks out at Area 51 were very surprised to see a Cessna landing at their secret base. They immediately impounded the aircraft and hauled the pilot into an interrogation room.

The pilot's story was that he took off from Vegas, got lost, and spotted the Base just as he was about to run out of fuel. The Air Force started a full FBI background check on the pilot and held him overnight during the investigation.

By the next day, they were finally convinced that the pilot really was lost and wasn't a spy. They gassed up his airplane, gave him a terrifying, "You didn't see a thing" briefing, complete with threats of life imprisonment, pointed him in the direction of Vegas and sent him on his way.

The next day, to the total disbelief of the Air Force, the same Cessna showed up again. Once again the MP's surrounded the plane … only this time there were two people in the plane.

The same pilot jumps out and says, "Do anything you want to me. Lock me up, throw away the key, ANYTHING you want! My wife is in the plane with me and you have GOT to tell her where I was last night."

5.   You walk in on your sweetie having sex with your best friend.

6.   You are served with divorce papers!!

7.   You see scratches on his back (and you didn't put them there).

8.   You start auditing his cell phone bill to see who he has been talking to.

Celebration

A man and his wife walk into a night club and spot a girl sitting at the bar alone. The husband says, "See that lady over there at the bar. That's my first girlfriend. She's been drinking since I left her 10 years ago." The wife replies, "Nonsense, no one celebrates that long."

Hell

A young lady comes home from a date looking rather sad. She tells her mother, "John proposed to me an hour ago."

Her mother asks, "Then why do you look so sad?"

The daughter said, "Because he told me he was an atheist and he doesn't believe there is a Hell."

Her mother replies, "Marry him anyway. Between the two of us, we'll show him how wrong he is!"

9.   He gets a new phone number and doesn't bother to tell you what it is.

10.   His penis doesn't get hard anymore when you touch it.

11.   He no longer performs oral sex on you. (When he stops eating your coochie, it's time to go.)

12.   You no longer kiss each other goodbye.

Good Education

A guy noticed that his buddy was troubled and asked what was wrong.

Guy: "Ohhh, it's my girlfriend."

Friend: "So what's the problem?"

Guy: "When I asked her if she could learn to love me, she asked me how much I was willing to spend on her education."

Positions

A husband walks into the kitchen where his wife is standing and asks:

Husband: Shall we try a different position tonight?

Wife: That's a good idea. Why don't you stand by the sink and do the dishes and I'll sit on the couch, watch TV and fart.

13. When he no longer WANTS oral sex from you.

14. When he stops asking or caring how your day went.

15. While lying in bed, both of you go out of your way to avoid touching each other.

16. He files a restraining order against you.

The Perfect Girl

Joanne, is a 35-year-old, single lady. All her friends are married except her. One day one of her girlfriends asks, "What's the matter, are you looking for the perfect man? Are you that picky? Can't you find anyone you're compatible with?"

Joanne replies, "Every time I meet a nice guy that I like and take him home to meet my parents, my father doesn't like him. So I keep on looking."

Her girlfriend suggests, "Listen, why don't you find someone who is just like your dear old father?"

A couple weeks go by and Joanne runs into her girlfriend. Her girlfriend asks, "So Joanne, did you ever find that perfect guy yet? You know, one that's just like your father?"

Joanne shrugs her shoulders, "Yes I found someone just like my Dad. When I took him home, my father loved him and they became fast friends."

Her girlfriend replies, "That's great. Are you all engaged yet?"

Joanne says, "I'm afraid not. My mother can't stand him."

17.   He blocks all your emails.

18.   You have been sleeping on the couch for the past 6 months.

19.   He moves and doesn't bother to give you his new address.

20.   You are choking and he doesn't lift a finger to help you.

<u>100 Camels</u>

A married couple touring the Middle East sat outside a café waiting for their friends. A peddler approached them, his arm loaded with watches. After an impassioned sales plea yielded nothing, he asked where they were from. "America" the husband replied.

Looking at her dark hair and olive skin, the Arab responded, "She's not from the States." "Yes I am," said the wife. He pointed to her husband and asked her, "Is he your husband?" To which the wife replied, "Yes!"

The Arab turns to the husband and says, "Mister, I'll give you one hundred camels for her." The husband sat for a long, stunned silence before he replied, "She's not for sale."

After the salesman leaves, his angry wife asked, "What took you so long to answer?" The husband replied, "I was trying to figure out how I could get a hundred camels back to America!"

21.   You go out to dinner and he introduces you to his new girlfriend.

22.   When you start snooping around in his email to read his messages.

23.   He gets another woman pregnant while you are still a couple.

24.   On Valentine's Day, he gives you an eviction notice.

Who Wants To Be A Millionaire

A man and his wife were watching "Who Wants To Be A Millionaire" while in bed. She turns to him and says, "Do you want to have sex?"

"No!" he answers.

The wife then says, "Is that your final answer?"

"Yes!" he replies.

The wife then says, "I'd like to phone a friend."

25.   When his mother starts calling you a "Bitch".

26.   You start to refer to him as, "What's his face" in conversations.

27.   He revokes your remote control privileges to everything at his house (including the gate, garage, and the TV).

28.   Your initials have been removed from all the monogrammed towels at his house, leaving just the letter for his name.

An Expensive Date

A goodlooking couple is sitting in a very expensive restaurant reading a menu. The man turns to his date and asks her what she would like to eat.

Scanning the menu, the woman replies, "To begin, I'll have two Champagne Cocktails, then a dozen Oysters on Half Shell, Turtle Soup and Crab Cakes. As an entrée, I'll have New York Pepper Steak, Alfredo Fettuccine with Chicken plus a Grilled Chicken Caesar Salad. For dessert, just bring me one of everything on the dessert menu."

Somewhat surprised, not only by her appetite, but also by the cost, the gentleman asks, "Do you eat this well at home too?"

She replies, "Well no, but no one at my house wants to have sex with me."

29.   You come home and everything is cleaned out of the house!!

30.   You answer your sweetie's cell phone and hear another ladies' voice. (Hey Babe, don't forget to bring some extra Viagra when you come over tonight.")

31.   He starts calling you names like "Fat Pig," "Cow" or "Oink Oink".

32.   He asks you to give him back the keys to his house.

The Salesman

A salesman away from home for several weeks walks into a restaurant one morning and tells his waitress, "I want two eggs fried very hard, two pieces of toast burnt black and a cup of weak, lukewarm coffee."

"Are you sure?" the waitress asks.

The salesman replies, "Yes."

When his order is ready (to the salesman specification), the waitress brings it out and serves it to him. Before leaving she asks him, "Is there anything else?"

The salesman says, "Yes, I want you to sit down and nag the hell out of me. I'm homesick!"

33. You call your house and your name has been removed from the greeting on the answering machine.

34. He cancels all your joint credit card accounts and removes your name from the lease.

35. You come home and have to knock to get in because there is a new dead bolt lock on the door. (If you have to knock to get in your own house, it's time to go.)

36. You find a 'No Trespassing' sign on your side of the bed.

The Gambler

An avid gambler says to his friend, "To please my wife, I have given up drinking smoking and playing cards."

His friend says, "That must make her very happy."

The Gambler said, "No, it hasn't. Now every time she begins to talk to me, she can't think of anything to say!"

The Couple

A couple drove down a country road for several miles, not saying a word. An earlier discussion led to an argument and neither of them wanted to concede their position.

As they passed a barnyard of mules, jackasses and pigs, the husband asked sarcastically, "Relatives of yours?"

"Yep," the wife replied, "In-laws."

37. He gives you a bill for all the money he has ever spent on you during the relationship.

38. For your anniversary, he gives you a card with a picture of his new girl-friend in it.

39. You come home and find all your stuff scattered all over the front lawn.

40. One of your friends runs into him on a date with someone else.

Female Compassion!

A man was sitting on a blanket at the beach. He had no arms and no legs.

Three women walked past and felt sorry for the poor man.

The first woman said, "Have you ever had a hug?"
The man said "No," so she gave him a hug and walked on.

The second woman said, "Have you ever had a kiss?"
The man said, "No." So she gave him a kiss and walked on.

The third woman came to him and said, "Have you ever been fucked?" The fellow said "No."

She replied, "You will be when the tide comes in."

41.　He constantly refers to you as a "bitch" or "whore" in conversations.

42.　You find yourself on the TV show "CHEATERS" checking up on your man.

43.　His family stops calling to invite you over for the holidays.

44.　**He always takes a shower before he comes home every night.** (If a guy has to shower all the time before he comes home to his lady, he's doing more than working out at the gym.)

Choosing a wife

A man wanted to get married. He was having trouble choosing among three likely candidates. He gives each woman a present of $5,000 and watches to see what they do with the money.

The first woman does a total make over. She goes to a fancy beauty salon, gets her hair done, purchases new make up and buys several new outfits. Then she dresses up very nicely for the man. She tells him that she wants to be more attractive for him because she loves him so much. The man was impressed.

The second woman goes shopping to buy the man gifts. She gets him a new set of golf clubs, some new gizmos for his computer, and some expensive clothes. As she presents these gifts she tells him that she has spent all the money on him because she loves him so much. Again, the man is impressed.

The third invests the money in the stock market. She earns several times the $5,000. She gives him back his $5,000 and reinvests the remainder in a joint account. She tells him that she wants to save for their future because she loves him so much. Obviously, the man was impressed.

The man thought for a long time about what each woman had done with the money he'd given her. He then marries the one with the biggest boobs. Men are like that, you know.

There is more money being spent on breast implants and Viagra today than on Alzheimer's research. This means that by 2040, there should be a large elderly population with perky boobs, huge erections and absolutely no recollection of what to do with them.

45.   **He stops French kissing you.**

46.   **Orgasms become an individual sport.** (His attitude is, "I got mine, you get yours!")

47.   **He cleans out all the money in your joint savings account.**

48.   **During sex, he calls you by another female's name.** (Under no circumstances should this ever happen unless he is drunk. Then again, that's another reason to leave cause he's probably an alcoholic.)

The Explanation

A wife came home early and found her husband, Big Fran, in their bedroom making love to a very attractive young woman. The wife was somewhat upset. "You are a disrespectful pig!" she cried. "How dare you do this to me—a faithful wife, the mother of your children! I'm leaving you. I want a divorce right away!"

Her husband replied, "Hang on just a minute my luv, so at least I can tell you what happened." "Fine, Go ahead", she sobbed, "but they will be the last words you'll say to me!"

Big Fran began, "Well, I was getting into the car to drive home and this young lady here asked me for a lift. She looked so down and out and defenseless that I took pity on her and let her into the car."

I noticed that she was very thin, not well dressed and very dirty. She told me that she hadn't eaten for three days! So, in my compassion, I brought her home and warmed up the enchiladas I made for you last night, the ones you wouldn't eat because you're afraid you'll put on weight. The poor thing devoured them in moments.

Since she needed a good clean-up, I suggested a shower and while she was doing that I noticed her clothes were dirty and full of holes so I threw them away. Then, I gave her the designer jeans that you have had for a few years, but don't wear because you say they are too tight.

Here Big Fran took a quick breath and continued—"She was so grateful for my understanding and help and as I walked her to the door she turned to me with tears in her eyes and said, "Please ... do you have anything else that your wife doesn't use?"

49. He permanently glues the toilet seat in the UP position.

50. He starts dating someone else who works in the same office as you.

51. He starts doing little things just to piss you off (standing you up for dates or shaving all the hair off his penis).

52. He starts stalking you everywhere you go.

The Young Train Conductor

A mother was working in the kitchen listening to her 5-year-old son playing with his new electric train in the living room. She heard the train stop and her son say, "All of you sons of bitches who want off, get the hell off now cause this is the last stop! And all of you sons of bitches who are getting on, get your asses on the train cause we're going on down the tracks."

The horrified mother went in and told her son, "We don't use that kind of language in this house. Now I want you to go to your room and you are to stay there for TWO HOURS. When you come out, you may play with your train but I want you to use nice language."

Two hours later, the son came out of the bedroom and resumed playing with his train. Soon the train stopped and the mother heard her son say. "All passengers, please remember your things, thank you and I hope your trip was a pleasant one. We hope you will ride with us again soon."

She heard her little darling continue. "For those of you just boarding, remember, there is no smoking on the train. We hope you will have a pleasant and relaxing journey with us today." As the mother began to smile, the child added, "For those of you who are pissed off about the TWO HOUR delay, Please see the bitch in the kitchen."

53. **You're no longer allowed to come over to his home.**

54. **While he is at home, you show up at his house unannounced but he refuses to answer the door.** (He is entertaining more than job offers when this happens. Can we say strippers & ho's?)

55. **After every date with you, he starts going home instead of spending the night with you** (like he is accustomed to doing).

56. **You find out that he is married.** (Self-explanatory)

The Secret To A Flat Tummy

A little boy walks into his parents' room to see his mom on top of his dad bouncing up and down.

The mom sees her son and quickly dismounts, worried about what her son has seen; she dresses quickly and goes to find him.

The son sees his mom and asks, "What were you and dad doing?"

The mother replies "Well you know your dad has a big tummy and sometimes I have to get on top of it to help flatten it."

"You're wasting your time." say's the boy.

"Why is that?" asks his mom, with a puzzled look on her face.

"Well when you go shopping, the lady next door comes over and gets on her knees and blows it right back up".

57.   He refuses to have sex with you face-to-face anymore because he doesn't want to look at your face.

58.   He stops returning your calls within a 24-hour period.

59.   You are traveling far from home and you go into a store to buy something. When you come back out, your partner is gone and your bags are sitting on the sidewalk.

60.   All your bathroom toiletries and other personal stuff at his place are moved from the cabinet into a 99¢ Store plastic bag hanging on the front door.

Mexican Style

A Mexican from El Paso found himself in Lubbock and decided to approach a prostitute down on 17th and R Streets.

He asked her, "How much do you charge for the hour?"

"$100," she replied.

"Do you do Messican-style?" he asked.

Not knowing exactly what this was, she refused. He tried to sweeten the deal and said, "I'll pay you $300 to do it Messiccan-style." Again she declined.

Being the persistent type, he laid down a final offer. "I'll give you $500 to go Messican-style with me! What do you say?" Finally, she agrees, thinking, "Well I've been in the game for over ten years now. I've been there and done that and had every kind of request from weirdoes from all over the world. How kinky could Messican-style be?"

After an hour of every possible way and position, she turned to him and said, "That was fantastic, but I was expecting something perverted and disgusting. Where does the 'Messican-style' come in?"

The Mexican popped a can of beer and replied, "I pay you next Wednesday when I get my check."

61. **He keeps making up excuses not to see you anymore.** (For example; I have to work late for the next 12 months or My dog is allergic to you.)

62. **You notice "hickies" on his neck and you didn't put them there.** (Self-explanatory)

63. **Every time you try to schedule time to go do something with him he says,** "I already have plans."

64. **He comes home drunk smelling like perfume and says that he was entertaining clients.** (What clients and what do these clients look like?)

My Wife Left Me

After our last child was born, she told me we had to cut back on expenses and I had to give up drinking beer.

I was not a big drinker, maybe a 12-pack on weekends.

Anyway, I gave it up but I noticed the other day when she came home from grocery shopping, the receipt included $45 for makeup.

Husband: "Wait a minute I've given up beer and you haven't given up anything!"

Wife: "I buy that makeup for you, so I can look pretty for you."

Husband: "Hell, that's what the beer was for!"

Husband: I don't think she'll be back.

65. You ask him how he's doing and he responds, "None of your damn business?"

66. He keeps hinting that "You" should start seeing other people.

67. He stops acknowledging important dates relating to you. (Such as your birthdays and Valentines Day and then he refuses to spend them with you.)

68. He starts ignoring your calls when your number shows up in his Caller ID.

Sex Life

Ramona: I don't know why people are always complaining about their sex life after they get married. Married people can have terrific sex.

Julie: Oh really? How is that?

Ramona: Well, look at me. I have a terrific sex life. It's not with my husband but it's terrific.

For Love or Money?

One summer morning, a husband turns to his wife and says, "It's just too hot to wear clothes today." As he stepped out of the shower he asks. "Honey, what do you think the neighbors will say if I mowed the lawn naked like this?"

With out missing a beat, his wife replied, "They'll probably say that I married you for your money."

69. You find a pair of female thongs under his bed (and they are not yours.)

70. You have to go through his secretary to talk to him on the phone.

71. You haven't spoken to each other in months.

72. He starts hanging out with his ex-girlfriend (or your ex-boyfriend for that matter).

7 Kinds of Sex

Recent research shows that there are 7 kinds of sex:

1. Smurf Sex: This kind of sex happens when you first meet someone and you both have sex until you are blue in the face.

2. Kitchen Sex: This is when you have been with your partner for a short time and you are so horny you will have sex anywhere, even in the kitchen.

3. Bedroom Sex: This is when you have been with your partner for a long time. Your sex has gotten routine and you usually have sex only in your bedroom.

4. Hallway Sex: This is when you have been with your partner for too long. When you pass each other in the hallway you both say, "Fuck you!"

5. Religious Sex: This means the man gets Nun in the morning, Nun in the afternoon and Nun at night.

6. Courtroom Sex: This is when the wife cannot stand her husband anymore. She takes him to court and screws him out of everything he owns in front of everyone.

7. Social Security Sex: The guy gets a little from time-to time, but not enough to live on.

73. He prefers to go to work at a job he hates rather than stay home and spend quality time with you. (If he always have to work on your birthday, Valentine's Day, Christmas, etc, he obviously doesn't want to be with you.)

74. You catch yourself doing stupid stuff like driving around late at night looking for him all over town.

75. He stops showing up for dates and don't bother to call and tell you he can't make it.

76. He starts making threats to commit physical violence against you.

Marriage Certificate

A husband and wife were quarreling for a while. After the cool down period, the husband came back to the wife in the morning and asked, "Honey, what are you doing?"

Trying to hide the document in her hand, the wife mumbled, "Nothing."

Noticing it is their marriage license, the husband burst into a verbal tirade, "I notice that you stayed up all night going over our marriage license with a fine-tooth comb examining every inch of it with a magnifying glass and you have the nerve to stand here in front of me and tell me that you weren't doing anything?"

Feeling dejected and somewhat embarrassed, the wife said, "All I was doing with our marriage license was looking to see if there was an expiration date on it."

77.   **You find out he lives with another woman.** (And she is not his mother, sister or daughter)

78.   **He quits his job and expects you to take care of him.** (Can we say LOSER!)

79.   **He starts coming home late every single night of the week and he doesn't even have a job.** (This is a sure sign that he is creeping with someone else)

80.   **You find yourself staying up late at nights wondering "Where he's at" and "Who is he with."** (This is not good for your sanity.)

My Harley

This guy has always dreamed of owning a Harley Davidson. One day he has finally saved up enough money so he goes down to the dealer. After he picks out the perfect bike, the dealer tells him about an old biker trick that will keep the chrome on his new bike free from rust.

The dealer tells him that all he has to do is to keep a jar of Vaseline handy and put it on the chrome before it rains, and everything will be fine. He happily pays for the bike and leaves. A few months later, the young man meets a woman and falls in love. She asks him to come home and meet her parents over dinner.

He readily accepts and the date is set. At the appointed time, he picks her up on his Harley and they ride to her parent's house. Before they go in, she tells him that they have a family tradition that whoever speaks first after dinner must do the dishes.

After a delicious dinner everyone sits in silence waiting for the first person to break the silence and get stuck doing the dishes. After a long fifteen minutes, the young man decides to speed things up, so he reaches over and kisses his woman in front of her family. No one says a word.

Emboldened, he slips his hand under her blouse and fondles her breasts. Still no one says a word. Finally, he throws her on the table and has sex with her in front of everyone. No one says a word. Now he is getting desperate, so he grabs her mother and throws her on the table. They have even wilder sex. Still no one speaks.

By now he is thinking what to do next when he hears thunder in the distance. His first thought is to protect the chrome on his Harley, so he gets his jacket, reaches in his pocket and pulls out his jar of Vaseline.

Right then the father says, "Okay, okay, I'll do the dishes!"

81. You have to take sleeping pills to go to sleep because he keeps stressing you out. (It's time to pack your shit and leave.)

82. He deletes all your numbers out of his cell phone.

83. You start thinking to yourself, "I wish he would go out and get a new girl-friend."

84. He tells you that he's working late at the office, but when you drop by to bring him dinner, he's not there.

Alimony

A woman wanting to get divorce from her rich husband visits an attorney. The attorney, trying to get the biggest possible alimony and settlement asks her, "Does he beat you?"

Woman: No, he doesn't.

Attorney: Does he hold back money from you?

Woman: No he does not.

Attorney: Is he an alcoholic?

Woman: No.

Getting frustrated from her answers, the attorney throws his hand up in the air and asks, "Is he unfaithful to you?"

The Woman is so excited that she shouts, "Yes, we got him on that count. He doesn't know this but he isn't the father of my two children."

85.   You find someone else's lipstick on his shirt collar.

86.   You start calling other women's cell phones looking for him.

87.   Your phone calls are returned a week after you leave the message.

88.   He deletes you from his speed dial.

The Burglar

A man goes to the police station wishing to speak to the burglar who had broken into his house the previous night. When he tells this to the police sergeant sitting behind the desk, the sergeant replies, "You'll get your chance to do so in court."

The man replies, "No, no, no, you don't understand. I simply want to ask him how he was able to get into my house without waking my wife. I've been trying to do that for the last 20 years."

The Scale

After the Holidays and all those delightful, seasonal treats, a husband stepped on one of those penny scales that tells your fortune and weight. He drops a coin and eagerly reads the results.

Husband: Listen to this, Honey. It says I'm energetic, bright, resourceful and an absolutely great lover in bed!

Wife: Yeah, and it has your weight wrong too!

89. He stops coming home at night.

90. He stops giving you compliments.

91. He starts dating other people and never bothers to tell you.

92. You bust out all his car windows and create a major scene by pushing on the car horn because you spot his car parked in another woman's driveway at 2 o'clock in the morning.

The Rolls Royce

A 16 year old boy drove into the driveway with a new Rolls Royce. His parents take one look at the car and proceed to ask the boy where he got the car?

The boy calmly replies, "I bought it with my allowance for $20."

With a look of disbelief on their face, the parents ask, "Who would sell you a Rolls Royce for $20?"

The boy says, "The lady up the street. I don't know her name, but she saw me riding my bike by her house and she asked me if I wanted to buy a car for $20."

The father says, "Something isn't right here. I'm going to go check this out."

The dad proceeds to walk over to the lady's house and have a chat. When the Dad gets there, he sees the lady calmly working in her garden.

Dad: Did you sell a Rolls Royce to my son for $20?

Lady: I sure did.

Dad: Really? Why?

Lady: Well, this morning I got a phone call from my husband. I thought he was away on a business trip, but last night I learned from a friend that he ran off to Hawaii with his secretary and didn't intend to come back. He told me that he was stranded, needed money right away and I should sell his new Rolls Royce and send him the money. So I did.

93.   You receive a cease and desist letter from his attorney about contacting him.

94.   As you approach the fridge its says "STEP AWAY FROM THE APPLI-ANCE YOU FAT PIG"

95.   You find a "Thinking About You" card from another woman on his dresser.

96.   All your pictures are removed from around his home.

The Hypnotist

A woman comes home from the hypnotist and tells her husband: "Remember those headaches I've been having all these years? Well, they're gone."

Husband: No more headaches? Well, that is wonderful.

Wife: You know, you haven't been exactly a ball of fire in the bedroom these last few years. Why don't you see the hypnotist and see if he can do anything for that?

The husband agrees to it. Following his appointment, the husband comes home, rips off his clothes, picks up his wife and carries her into the bedroom. He puts her on the bed and says, "Don't move. I'll be right back." He goes into the bathroom and comes back a few minutes later and jumps into bed and makes passionate love to his wife like never before.

Wife: Boy that was wonderful.

Husband: Don't move! I'll be right back.

He goes back into the bathroom, comes back and round two was even better that the first time. The wife sits up and her head is spinning. Her husband tells her not to move again, that he'll be right back. Then he runs into the bathroom.

This time, his wife quietly follows him and there in the bathroom, she sees him standing at the mirror saying: "She's not my wife. She's not my wife. She's not my wife."

97. He removes all his clothes from your home without telling you why.

98. You call him several times late at night and he doesn't answer his phone, but the next day he says he was sleeping and didn't hear his phone ringing.

99. He is always talking about you like you're a past memory. (For example: "Remember how much fun we used to have?" "Remember when we used to be together?")

100. None of his future plans seem to involve you anymore.

Killing Me Softly

A doctor was addressing a large audience in Tampa.

The material we put into our stomachs is enough to have killed most of us sitting here years ago. Red meat is awful. Soft drink corrodes your stomach lining. Chinese food is loaded with MSG. High fat diets can be disastrous and none of us realize the long-term harm caused by the germs in our drinking water. But there is one thing that is the most dangerous of all and we will have or will eat it.

"Can anyone here tell me what food it is that causes the most grief and suffering years after eating it?"

After several seconds of silence, a 75-year old woman in the front row raised her hand and said softly, "Wedding cake."

101. He gives you the classified ads with potential apartments circled.

102. You catch him responding to several personal ads on the internet. (If he has a Myspace account and it's not for business purposes, it's time to go! More than likely he's on there picking up girls.)

103. You ask him for his new home phone number and he tells you that he doesn't have one.

104. He asks for the engagement ring that he gave you.

Rest In Peace

When the rich man's will was read, his wife was very upset that he left everything to the young woman who lived next door and nothing to her.

She immediately drove down to the cemetery to cancel her order for his headstone.

The stone-carver tells her, "You're too late. I already carved it just like you told me: 'Rest In Peace'." The woman thought for a moment and then replies, "Okay, then I'll pay a little more to add, 'Till we meet again!'"

Country Funeral

A wonderful funeral was in progress and the country preacher talked at length of the good traits of the deceased, "What an honest man he was, and what a loving husband and kind father he was."

Finally the widow leaned over and whispered to one of her children, "Go up there and take a look in the coffin and see if that's your father."

105. Your perfumes are removed from his bathroom.

106. He removes your name from his health & car insurance. (Nothing says it's really over like getting sick, going to the doctor and finding out you were removed from his health insurance six months ago.)

107. You find out that he is gay. (Ladies, you have to watch out for the down low-guys that pretend to like women but they are really into men).

108. You find out that he is bi-polar schizophrenic.

Baked Beans

One day I met a sweet gentleman and fell in love. When it became apparent that we would marry, I made "The" supreme sacrifice and gave up beans.

Some months later on my birthday, my car broke down on the way home from work. Since I lived in the countryside, I called my husband and told him that I would be late because I had to walk home.

On my way home, I passed by a small diner and the odor of baked beans was more than I could stand. With miles to walk, I figured I would walk off any ill effects by the time I reached home, so I stopped at the diner and before I knew it, I had consumed three large orders of baked beans.

All the way home, I made sure that I released all the gas. Upon my arrival, my husband seemed excited to see me and exclaimed, delightedly, "Darling, I have a surprise for dinner tonight."

He then blindfolded me and led me to my chair at the dinner table. I took a seat, and just as he was about to remove my blindfold, the telephone rang. He made me promise not to touch the blindfold until he returned and went to answer the call.

The baked beans I had consumed were still affecting me and the pressure was becoming most unbearable, so while my husband was out of the room I seized the opportunity, shifted my weight to one leg and let one go. It was not only loud, but it smelled like a fertilizer truck running over a skunk in front of a pulp-wood mill. I took my napkin from my lap and fanned the air around me vigorously. Then, shifting to the other cheek, I ripped off three more. The stink was worse than cooked cabbage.

Keeping my ears carefully tuned to the conversation in the other room, I went on like this for another few minutes. The pleasure was indescribable. Eventually, the telephone farewells signaled the end of my freedom, so I quickly fanned the air a few more times with my napkin, placed it on my lap and folded my hands back on it feeling very relieved and pleased with myself.

My face must have been the picture of innocence when my husband returned, apologizing for taking so long. He asked me if I had peeked through the blindfold, and I assured him I had not. At this point, he removed the blindfold, and twelve dinner guests seated around the table chorused: "Happy Birthday!"

I fainted!!!!!!!!!!!

109. You go to the ATM and your PIN number doesn't work on your joint account.

110. He stops calling you.

111. Your mailbox key does not work anymore.

112. **He starts acting funny whenever you are around him.** (For example, hanging up the phone, getting off the internet or speaking in hush tones on the phone).

75 Years Together

An elderly couple is having an elegant dinner to celebrate their 75th wedding anniversary.

The old man leans forward and says softly to his wife, "Dear, there is something that I must ask you. It has always bothered me that our 10th child never quite looked like the rest of our children. Now I want to assure you that these 75 years have been the most wonderful experience I could have ever hoped for and your answer cannot take all that away. But I have to know, "Did he have a different father?"

The wife drops her head, unable to look her husband in the eye. She pauses for a moment and then confesses, "Yes, yes he did."

The old man is shaken a bit. The reality of what his wife admitted hit him harder than he expected. With a tear in his eye he asks, "Who? Who was the father?"

Again, the old woman drops her head, saying nothing at first as she tries to muster the courage to tell the truth to her husband. Then finally she says, "You".

113. Both of you start dating other people.

114. He stops taking you with him to events.

115. You constantly argue.

116. The phone conversations between you and him have become very weak and strained.

A Soldier

A soldier came to a fork in the road and saw a nun standing there. Out of breath he asked, "Please Sister, may I hide under your shirt for a few minutes? I'll explain WHY later." The nun agreed.

Just a moment later, two Military Police came running along and asked, "Sister, have you seen a soldier running by here?"

The nun pointed and replied, "He went that way."

After the MP's disappeared, the soldier crawled out from under her skirt and said, "I can't thank you enough Sister, but you see I don't want to go fight in the war in Iraq."

The nun said, "I think I can fully understand your fear." The soldier added, "I hope you don't think me rude or impertinent, but you have a great pair of legs!"

The nun replied, "If you had looked a little higher, you would have seen a great pair of balls.... I don't want to go fight in the war in Iraq either."

117. When another woman starts answering his phone.

118. **You get into the biggest arguments over what you are going to eat.** ("Baby, I asked you what you wanted to eat for dinner and you said chicken. I cook chicken for you and now you want something else. If that's the attitude you're going to have, fix your own damn dinner then!")

119. He ignores you when he sees you out in public.

120. **You no longer have freaky or romantic sex, just regular sex.** (For example after he gets oral sex from you he rolls over and goes right to sleep).

Communication

A judge was interviewing a woman regarding her pending Divorce.

Judge: What are the grounds for your divorce?

Lady: About four acres and a nice little home in the middle of the property with a stream running by.

Judge: No. I mean what is the foundation of this case?

Lady: It is made of concrete, brick and mortar.

Judge: I mean, what is your relationship like?

Lady: I have an aunt and uncle living here in town and so do my husband's parents.

Judge: Do you have a real grudge?

Lady: No. We have a two-car carport and have never really needed one.

Doctor: Please, is there any infidelity in your marriage?

Lady: Yes. Both my sons have stereo sets. We don't necessarily like the music, but the answer to your question is yes.

Judge: Ma'am, does your husband ever beat you?

Lady: Yes. About twice a week he gets up earlier than I do.

Finally, in frustration the judge asks;

Judge: Lady, why do you want a divorce?

Lady: Oh, I don't want a divorce. I've never wanted a divorce. My husband does. He said he couldn't communicate with me!

121. You feel absolutely nothing inside for this person anymore.

122. He starts writing his name on everything he owns or buys in the home that you share together.

123. He draws a "Do Not Cross" line in the middle of the apartment or house that you share together.

124. When you start asking yourself that question, "I wonder if this relationship is over?" (It's over!)

The Prescription

A lady went to a pharmacy, walked right up to the pharmacist, looked straight into his eyes, and said, "I would like to buy some cyanide."

The pharmacist asked, "Why in the world do you need cyanide?"

The lady replied, "I need it to poison my husband."

The pharmacist's eyes got big and he exclaimed, "Lord have mercy! I can't give you cyanide to kill your husband! That's against the law! I'll lose my license! They'll throw both of us in jail! All kinds of bad things will happen. Absolutely not! You CANNOT have any cyanide!"

The lady reached into her purse and pulled out a picture of her husband in bed with the pharmacist's wife.

The pharmacist looked at the picture and replied, "Well now, that's different. You didn't tell me you had a prescription."

125. He volunteers to go to Iraq for an unspecified amount of time to fight in the war just to get the hell away from you.

126. You call his house phone, cell phone and work numbers and the only voice you hear is the operator stating, "the phone number you dialed has been disconnected and there is no new number ..."

127. He starts calling you much less than he use to in the past.

128. You regularly attend Sunday dinner with the family, but when you go this one particular Sunday, there's a sign posted in the window with your name on it written in large red bold letters followed by: "No Visitors Allowed, the relationship is over!" (No further explanation should be needed, especially if you were always the only non-family member at the dinner table.)

A Bottle of Wine

A gentleman asked a waiter to take a bottle of Chardonnay over to an attractive woman.

The waiter took the wine to the woman and said, "This is from the gentleman seated over there," indicating the sender.

She regarded the wine coolly for a second, not looking at the man, and decided to send a reply note to the man.

The waiter, who was lingering for a response, took the note from her and conveyed it to the gentleman.

The note read:

"For me to accept this bottle, you need to have a Mercedes in your garage, a million dollars in the bank, and 7 inches in your pants."

After reading the note, the man decided to compose one of his own in return.

He folded the note, handed it to the waiter and instructed him to return this to the woman.

It read: "For your information, I have a Ferrari Maranello, a BMW Z8, a Mercedes CL600 and a Porsche Turbo in my garage. There are over twenty million dollars in my bank account, but not even for a woman as beautiful as you, would I cut off three inches.

Just send the damn bottle back. Thank you."

129. When he's not around, everyday is Drama Free Day.

130. Little things about him that never use to bother you, start bothering you. (Him—hanging out with his male friends, burping and not covering his mouth, scratching his butt and farting in the bed at night)

131. The double sink is removed from the bathroom at the home you share together.

132. Even though you live together, you have to start going to the grocery store and buying your own groceries.

The Golfer

A golfer was involved in a terrible car crash and was rushed to the hospital. Just before he was put under, the surgeon popped in to see him.

Surgeon: I have some good news and bad news! The bad news is that I have to remove your right arm!

Man: O God, no! My golfing is over! Please Doc, what's the good news?

Doctor: The good news is, I have another one to replace it with, but it's a woman's arm. I'll need your permission before I go ahead with the transplant.

Man: Go for it doc! As long as I can play golf again.

The operation went well and a year later the man was out on the golf course when he bumped into the surgeon.

Doctor: Hey, how's the new arm?

Man: Just great! I'm playing the best golf of my life. My new arm has much finer touch and my putting has really improved.

Doctor: That's great.

Man: Not only that, my handwriting has improved. I've learned how to sew my own clothes and I've even taken up painting landscapes in watercolors.

Doctor: Unbelievable! I'm so glad to hear the transplant was such a great success. Are you having any side effects?

Man: Well, there is just one problem. Every time I get in a loving mood and want to have sex, I also get a headache.

133. He starts comparing you to his ex-girlfriends during every argument. ("Tiffany's meatloaf tasted better than yours." or "You are crazy just like my ex-Joanne.")

134. He talks about getting too many calls on his cell phone even though he told you he didn't have one.

135. You have to repeatedly call him to see if he got your messages that you left on his voicemail cause he never bothers to return your calls anymore.

136. You can no longer access your voicemail on the home phone because the password has been changed.

The Check

A husband goes to Europe and calls his wife. While talking to her on the phone, he says to her, "I sent you a cheque of countless hugs and kisses. Did you receive it?"

The wife says, "I did and I cashed it with our next door neighbor."

Hurry Up and Wait

A husband sitting downstairs waiting in his living room shouts out to his wife.

Husband: For the Last time, are you ready to go?

Wife: For Heaven's sake, be quiet. I've been telling you for the last hour and a half, that I'll be ready in minute.

137. **He starts making up excuses not to sleep with you anymore.** (He says to you, "You're not going to believe this, but it's that time of month so we can't do anything.")

138. **When a moving truck pulls up in your driveway and starts packing up all your stuff without your knowledge.**

139. **All of a sudden, he starts stocking perfumed shower gel in his bathroom.** (And it's not for you. Who the heck is showering in his bathroom when you are not around? hmmmmm)

140. **He's always talking to you about the great times he has at parties he never bothers to invite you to.**

Aspirin

A husband emerged from the bathroom naked and was climbing into bed when his wife complained, as usual, "I have a headache."

"Perfect," her husband said. "I was just in the bathroom powdering my penis with aspirin. You can take it orally or as a suppository—it's up to you."

The Betrayal

Doctor Dave had slept with one of his patients and felt guilty all day long. No matter how much he tried to forget about it, he just couldn't.

The guilt and sense of betrayal was overwhelming. But every once in a while, he'd hear an internal, reassuring voice in his head that said,

"Dave, don't worry about it. You aren't the first medical practitioner to sleep with one of his patients and you won't be the last. Besides, you're single so just let it go, Dave."

But invariably another voice in his head would bring him back to reality, whispering,

"Dave....

        Dave....

                Dave....

You're a Veterinarian, you sick bastard".

141   He turns off his cell phone every time you're around.

142. The passenger seat is removed from the family car.

143. He starts berating you in public as if you're his child.

144. He tells you that you're his property and you better do as he say or else …

The Ultimate Pre-Marital Test—(true story)

I was a very happy person. My wonderful girlfriend and I had been dating for over two years and we decided to get married. There was only one thing bothering me: her beautiful younger sister. My sister-in-law-to-be was twenty-two, wore very tight miniskirts and went bra-less. One day she called and asked me to come over to check the wedding invitations.

She was alone when I arrived, and she told me she had feelings and desires for me that she couldn't overcome. She said she wanted to make love to me just once before I married her sister.

Of course I was totally shocked and couldn't say a word. She said, "I'm going upstairs to my bedroom, but if you want one last wild fling, come up and join me." I was stunned as I watched her go up the stairs. At the top, she pulled off her panties and threw them down at me.

I stood there for a moment then turned and made a beeline straight out the front door to my car. Lo and behold, my entire future family was standing outside, all clapping! With tears in his eyes, my future father-in-law to be hugged me and said, "We're so happy that you've passed our little test. We couldn't ask for a better man for our daughter. Welcome to the family."

The moral of this story is: "Guys should always keep their condoms in their car."

145. Instead of butterflies in your stomach when you see him, you are overcome with nausea.

146. Your mutual friends start sending both of you separate invitations to all their parties.

147. The utility bills start coming to you in 2 parts ... his and hers.

148. He spends hours chatting online rather than talking to you.

149. You find yourself constantly making pros & cons list regarding his good and bad qualities. (Pros—good credit, nice car, good job.... Con—bad breath, shitty attitude, little penis ...)

The following is a survey I took that I thought was very interesting. I have replaced the names of the person that said it with their gender to protect their identity.

FOUR WORDS TO SAY AFTER SEX:

1. The bitch burnt me—guy
2. I need a cigarette—lady
3. Wow that was great—guy
4. Where are my clothes?—lady
5. I say goddamn!—lady
6. Fuck, who are you?—guy
7. Shit, my wife's home—guy
8. Let's do it again!!—lady
9. I'm Rick James, Bitch.—guy
10. Really, is that it???—lady
11. Thanks baby, good night!!!—guy
12: That'll be 500 dollars—lady
13. See, size does matter!!—lady
14. Next time hit record!!—guy
15. Okay roll over, Bedtime—guy
16. You can leave now—guy
17. Pass me that towel—guy
18. Make me a sandwich—guy
19. Let's smoke that blunt!—lady
20. Damn! you're a quickie—lady
21. I'm glad you're satisfied!!!—lady
22. I beat that up—guy
23. Awww shit it broke!!!!—lady
24. You walking kinda funny?—guy
25. If I only knew!!??—lady
26. I have had better!!!!—guy
27. What's your name again??—guy
28. I hit your cervix!—guy
29. Cut! That's a wrap!—guy
30. That was fuckin' AMAZING!!—lady

FOUR WORDS TO SAY AFTER SEX—continued

31. Was That Round Five?—lady
32. Tell your mom, hi.—guy
33. High five on that—guy
34. Go out the window—guy
35. Sleep on the couch—lady
36. Where did it go?—lady
37. Send your sister in.—guy
38. Okay, it's hard again—guy
39. I need another condom—lady
40. Was that your eye?—guy
41. My sinuses are clear!!—lady
42. Damn! That sure sucked!!—guy
43. Thanks, now get out!—lady
44. Did you lose it?—lady
45. That was way unexpected!—guy
46. Who's your daddy bitch—guy
47. We need new sheets—guy
48. I was almost there—lady
49. I wanna go home—lady
50. Get in the shower!!!—lady
51. What's ya name again?—lady
52. Can you go again?—lady
53. Here's some bus fare—guy
54. Are You Fuckin Serious!—lady
55. That Lexus ain't MINE!!!!—guy
56. Get me a baby wipe—lady
57. Don't love me ok?—lady
58. IT'S RUDE TO SPIT!!!—guy
59. Time for round 2!!—guy
60. Ride me hard, stud!!—lady

5 KINGS

Below are five great Kings that has brought happiness to many peoples lives all over the world:

1. drinKING

2. smoKING

3. sucKING

4. licKING

5. fucKING

Afterword

It's nice to be important, but it's more important to be nice. Some of you ladies need to make better choices when selecting a man. If the relationship doesn't work out, it probably wasn't meant to be. Don't become bitter and start hating on men. Move on with your life and someone who is probably better for you will eventually come along. Don't go into the new relationship with baggage from the old one. No one wants to be with someone who is bitter or has a lot of baggage. My mother always told me, "You can catch more flies with honey than with vinegar." Whenever you start a new relationship and you will see how much of a difference one's attitude makes to a person of the opposite sex. Hopefully, this book has given many of you an inside peek at how a man really thinks. Keep the faith and don't stop loving. There is true love out there for everyone.

About the Author

Jeff Hodge—The following words were used to describe me in ONE WORD ... just one word by friends and co-workers: focused, kind innovative, responsible, funny, secretive, extroverted, cunning, friendly, enigmatic, hot, sincere, charismatic, persistent, mysterious, unpredictable, non-retarded, resourceful and sexy. For more information, visit my website at: www.jeffhodge.com or www.myspace.com/jeffhodgecomedian.

Other Books by Jeff Hodge

101+ Ways To Keep A Man—$15.00—A how-to guide instructing women about how men think and what they really want in a relationship. Real-life relationship advice in an easy to understand and execute manner. www.101waystokeepaman.com
ISBN: 0-595-37633-9

101+ Ways to Get Out f a Traffic Ticket—$10.00—A humorous book filled with lots of funny excuses and stories motorists have used over the years to get out of traffic tickets.
ISBN: 0-9633347-0-0

Pet Peeves: Things That Tick Me Off About Driving—$10.00—A humorous book that shows motorists how to deal with their pet peeves and road rage when they are behind the wheel.
ISBN: 0-9633347-5-1

101 Ways to Stay Awake When on the Road—$10.00—A humorous book that has funny takes on road signs and what they mean. It also gives readers creative ways to stay awake when they find themselves falling asleep behind the wheel.
ISBN: 0-9633347-1-9

Order your **autographed** copies now. Visit www.jeffhodge.com for more details or simply use the order form on the following page.

Order Form

Name: _____

Address: _____

City: _____ State: _____ Zip: _____

Name of title: _____

Number of copies _____   x   Price: _____

                                             Subtotal: _____

Shipping & Handling: $3.50

                                             Total: _____

Make money orders payable to: **Yeah Mon Entertainment** *
P.O. Box 88304 * Los Angeles, CA 90009-8304. Please allow
4–6 for weeks delivery.

978-0-595-42567-9
0-595-42567-4

www.ingramcontent.com/pod-product-compliance
Lightning Source LLC
Chambersburg PA
CBHW030411290526

45785CB00004B/1962